W9-ATH-693

Albert B. Cub

& Zebra

AN ALPHABET STORYBOOK

Anne Rockwell

A HARPER TROPHY BOOK

Harper & Row, Publishers

Library of Congress Cataloging in Publication Data Rockwell, Anne F. Albert B. Cub & Zebra. SUMMARY: The adventures of Albert B. Cub as he tries to find the culprits who abducted his beloved Zebra. [1. Alphabet books. 2. Stories without words.] I. Title. PZ7.R5943A1 [E] 76-54224 ISBN 0-690-01350-7 ISBN 0-690-01351-5 (lib. bdg.) "A Harper Trophy Book" ISBN 0-06-443140-1 (pbk.) Published in hardcover by Thomas Y. Crowell.

Aa

Bb

Cc

Dd

Ee

Ff

Gg

Hh

Ii

J j

K k

Ll

Mm

Nn

Oo

MARKET

EAT HAM

SPECIAL!
$1.69
per lb.

89¢

ONE WAY

Pp

Qq

Rr

Ss

Tt

Uu

Vv

Ww

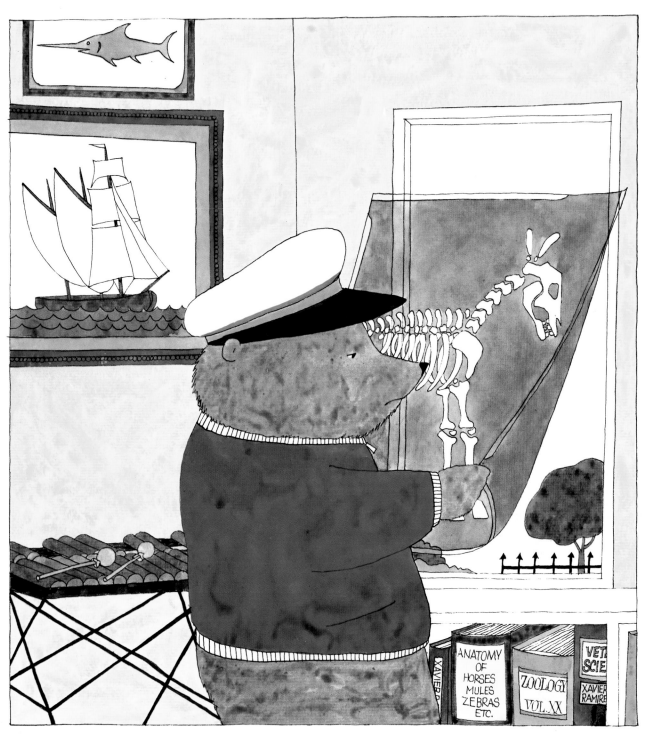

ANATOMY
OF
HORSES
MULES
ZEBRAS
ETC.

ZOOLOGY
VOL. XX

VET.
SCIE.

XAVIER
RAMIRE

Xx

Yy

Zz

Albert B. Cub & Zebra

*Some of the things in the alphabet pictures are named in
this story. Can you find more? You can look for them
while Albert looks for Zebra.*

Aa Albert B. Cub is riding on Zebra, past
an arcade formed of arches. Suddenly
Zebra is abducted! Albert falls; there is an ac-
cident with an automobile. Who took Zebra?
Only an arm shows. Under the arcade there is a
poster of an ape. A lady walking by has ankles.
An accountant has an office there. In the air an
airplane flies. A pilot is sometimes called an
aviator. An artist is absorbed in painting an
angel. He has other paintings. One is of a knight
in armor and one is of an alligator. An Angora
cat sees Albert fall. She knows Zebra's abductor.
An arrow points, but where? There are many
angles of varying degrees. A boy, eating an apple,
watches. He is carrying his arithmetic homework.
Some of it is addition. An Airedale stands along-
side him. A little girl is sobbing in anguish. Has
she had an argument with her friend? But the
squirrel nibbles his acorn. Do you see the amper-
sand in the accountant's sign?

Bb Albert B. Cub (the B. stands for Bern-
hardt), his leg bound with bandages, is
in a backyard. He is a brown bear. He is talking
with a St. Bernard and a basset. Neither knows
where Zebra is. A boy has a baseball and a bat. A
butterfly hovers over the bush. Some roses are in
blossom, others in bud. There is a bug and a bee.
A bird bathes in the birdbath. A boy is reading
a book. On the cover, a billy goat crosses a bridge.
A man with a beard and buttons on his shirt and
a band around his hat gardens. He has weeds in a
basket. He is bald and has a brow. A girl has
braids. A ball is on the grass and a barefoot boy
blows bubbles. Two children in bathing suits are
sailing a boat. It has a mast, a sail, and a boom.
The girl has bangs. One boy has a balloon, another has a box. Whose bicycle with brakes is

that? Does it belong to the lady who is baking
the pie? A milk bottle stands on the stoop. There
is a bell to ring. There are four burners on the
stove, a light bulb in the kitchen, and bananas in
the bowl. The house is made of bricks. The baby
is in bed. There is a bureau and a lamp with a
shade and a base. A bus goes by. It has bumpers.
It is painted blue and gray. The busdriver wears
a beige uniform. A blimp flies overhead. Perhaps
someone in the blimp has seen Zebra. Who
knows? The tree with bark, branches, and a bird-
house is silent; the dogs pant and bark hello, but
they are no help.

Cc Crying, carrying a cane with a crook,
and wearing his crimson jacket with
cuffs and his white cap, the poor cub goes to the
circus. The clown with circles on his suit and a
big collar and crosses across his eyes has not
seen Zebra. His mouth curves down in compas-
sion. Nor has the ringmaster, elegantly clad in
cape, cravat, and cummerbund. He is very hand-
some with his curly hair and mustache that curls
up in a crescent. He smokes a cigar, but he does
not know that a little caterpillar is crawling on
his top hat. Whose birthday is it? The cook carries a cake with candles. Or is he a chef? The
beautiful bareback rider wears a crown. A tramp
clown drives a little car. The tiger, who is a
carnivore with claws, is in the cage. The car-
penter is on his way to fix something. Crowds are
arriving. A little girl has cotton candy. A man
has a camera. The tents are made of canvas.
Bright colors are everywhere, but clouds are in
the sky.

Dd Days pass. Albert is better now and
still searches for Zebra. Here he is,
going out on a dock toward a dinghy. The Big

Dipper is in the sky because it is dark. It points in the direction of the North Star. The cottage has a door. Inside the house a daddy sits at his drawing table. He is wearing a derby hat and drawing a dinosaur. On the window sill there sits a duck but it is not real, only a decoy. Daisies are in the pot which has a diamond pattern. Baby is down on the floor in diapers, along with a doll in a dress with polka dots. The rug on the floor has a design. Two dogs drink from a dish. The dalmatian has a drop of water dripping from his tongue, but the dachshund is tidier. Mother, who is a dancer, is dancing, but soon she will pull the drapes and everyone will go to sleep. But will Albert sleep? Who knows?

Ee In a large department store, on the eighth floor, Albert sadly wanders. It is the toy floor. The elevator stops here; so does the escalator. The elevator operator has epaulettes on his uniform. Everyone has eyes and ears. One passenger wears eyeglasses and the young lady has earrings, espadrilles, and an embroidered shirt. A lady comes up the escalator. She must be rich, for she wears an ermine coat and an emerald ring. What toys she can buy! There is an Easter bunny with a basket of eggs. There is an elephant, an Eskimo doll, an elf, an engine, and a palace guard. He is an Englishman. Some toys are educational, such as a globe of the earth and an easel. But Albert wants none of them. Near the electrical outlet a boy eating a candy cane says hello, but Albert goes on without answering, for he still has not found Zebra. He must look elsewhere.

Ff How far Albert has come! He is in France, fishing for his dinner. A Frenchman waves to him. He has five fingers. Albert is furry and fat. A fly is on his hat. His line has a float. The fisherman has caught four fish. The duck has lost a feather. And Albert has lost Zebra. What a nice lunch the fisherman has, bread and wine, some fruit, and a knife and fork for eating. Butterflies flutter and fly about. Two boys are fighting. One has freckles. A little frog watches and waits. But see the sly fox! Will he steal a fish? All the people have faces. Flowers are growing. Albert is fifty kilometers from Paris, near a farm. The farmer pitches hay in his field; his wife will soon milk the cow. Wife and cow are both females. Far off, the French flag flies.

Gg Albert peeks in at a garden gate, but he does not see Zebra. A goat chews green grass Geraniums grow in big pots, and a goldfinch perches on the wall. Grapes grow on a grapevine, and gladioli shoot up from the ground. Goldfish are in the pond, and a garter snake is on the grass. A gray goose and gander and their three goslings are in the garden, and so is a girl. The girl is blowing bubble gum and carrying a gift and a book about ghosts. Is the gift for the gardener? There he kneels, with his gloves, galoshes, and galluses to hold his trousers up. He is wearing glasses. Does he see the grasshopper? Albert does, but it has not seen Zebra. The gardenias on the bush smell sweet, and Albert would like to linger but he must go.

Hh Here is Albert, half hidden behind a hedge. He is wearing his hat, and is in some danger of being stung on his black nose by a hornet. Hounds are baying as they hunt a fox. Horses follow, ridden by hunters and huntsmen with helmets on their heads and wearing riding habits. The hunters have hands to hold harnesses. The horses have hocks and hooves and they wear horseshoes. One huntsman blows a horn, "Ta-Tay, Ta-Tay." A hen struts up a hill; a hedgehog and a hare run from a hawk. On a higher hill a farmer hoes, and his wife, in a dress covered with hearts, rests with her hands on her hips. A boy holds a stick to roll his hoop. There is a pitchfork in the haystack, a rabbit in a hutch, and a hog on the lawn. The house is the farm family's home. Why is that helicopter or Hovercraft hovering overhead? Does it bring news of Zebra to Albert B. Cub?

Ii On a slowly moving iceberg, Albert kneels. An Imperial tern keeps him company. To pass the time, Albert takes the dimensions of the iceberg. He writes with ink and measures feet and inches. A walrus, with tusks of ivory, stares at him. An Eskimo paddles by in a kayak. His parka has a design of isosceles triangles. An igloo made of ice stands isolated on a little island, or isle. It is home for the Eskimo, but Zebra has never been there.

Jj Albert is in the jungle. He arrived by jeep #J-1966120. Why is he wearing a jacket when it is so hot? Albert is relaxing on his long journey by playing jacks. Soon he will eat his lunch. Although bears prefer honey, Albert will have to settle for jellybeans, jam and jelly, and juice from the jug. A jabiru with a jolly smile wades in the river. Albert does not see the jaguar resting in the tree. Perhaps Zebra is hidden in the jungle somewhere, but I don't see him. Do you?

Kk Whose kitchen is this? It must belong to the king. The king is cutting kohlrabi with a knife. He is cooking something containing kernels of corn, ketchup, and knockwurst. Perhaps kidney beans will be included, for the cook is bringing some in a bowl. A picture of a kangaroo is on the cookbook. A kettle is on the stove. A key is on a hook and a keyhole is under the knob on the door. Someone's knitting is in the basket. Who is the little girl in the knotted kerchief, wearing a knapsack and kissing a kitten? Is she the little princess, or the cook's daughter? A kid, perhaps her brother, is in a tree. He is wearing knickers. A kite flies over a kiosk, but nobody knows where Zebra is. Albert B. Cub paddles a kayak swiftly down the river, still searching for him. Do you suppose the Eskimo gave Albert the kayak?

Ll Albert is in the living room of a friendly family who has given him lodging for the night. He is licking a lemon lollipop. He holds it with his right paw, not his left. A girl with long locks of hair and wearing a leotard that covers her legs is lying down and listening to his story. Her brother is sitting in a ladderback chair looking at his lessons. His paper has lines. The lamp is lighted. He has taken off his sneakers, the laces are untied. The door has a lock. Two lovebirds are in a cage. A lady, she must be the mother, is sitting in a chair. She has lovely lashes and lips, and she wears lace on her sleeves and a locket around her neck. Sitting on her lap there is a little boy. He is looking at a book. A spotted leopard is on the cover. Perhaps there is a picture of a zebra in the book, but it is not Albert B. Cub's friend. Does the hook and ladder on the floor belong to big brother, little brother, or sister? Logs are burning in the fireplace, which has a lozenge carved on it. On the mantel a lizard lives on a log of driftwood. Lilacs with leaves are in the pitcher. The walls have pictures. One is a landscape. In another picture, the lion lies down with the lamb. In another, a lighthouse beams its welcoming, luminous light to the sailboat. What a nice place this would be to linger, but Albert must leave tomorrow.

Mm Albert has come many miles to Maine. The moon is up above the mountain. A martin flies. A moose, with a morose expression, looks out from behind a tree. A motorcycle with a motor is there. Does it belong to Albert or to the man putting a marshmallow in his mouth? I hope that doesn't make his mustache sticky. He has money and a map and a maroon jacket. He travels with his monkey and they put on shows. He saw Albert's zebra once, but that was long ago and far away. It is chilly in Maine and Albert wears a muffler, but he has taken off his mittens. There are many mammals here, including Albert, the man, the moose, the mouse, and the mink. Mushrooms grow in the forest. Albert lighted the fire with matches. Besides marshmallows, Albert has milk and hot dogs made of meat, smeared with mustard. He has a magazine to read. It has a picture of a Martian on the cover. Oh my, will Albert go to Mars to look for his friend Zebra?

Nn No, Albert has not gone to Mars. He is crossing Niagara Falls. He looks nervous. A nighthawk flies. A nymphalid butterfly will not be caught in the butterfly net, for its owner is napping. He has a neckerchief; his compass points north and there are notes on his music. The night heron does not notice the nickel lying next to the falls. Are the people near the fir tree newlyweds? The man is reading the newspaper. It is full of news. The woman neatly wipes her mouth with a napkin, and soon she will knit with her needles. A squirrel is eating a nut.

Oo Albert's odyssey continues. He is in an oxcart, pulled by a yoke of oxen. They wear an oxbow and one ox is eating some oats. An osprey has caught a fish. The fisherman has caught many fish, and also an octopus. Every day the fisherman goes out in his boat called "Olympia" and puts his oars in the oarlocks and fishes. I doubt if he has seen Zebra. The little boy has a toy orangutan. The woman walking on the shore by the ocean has a basket of okra on her head and a basket of onions in her hands. An olive tree grows and in its shade an oboist plays her oboe. In the distance stands an obelisk, and a church with an oculus and an ogive arch in the tower. A goose has just laid an oval egg, and is standing over it. A man goes down the steps. Perhaps he will lend Albert B. Cub his opera glasses to look for Zebra. The shop is number three. Three is an odd number. In the shop an oculist, or optometrist, sells glasses. His name is Otto. An old lady snoozes in the sun. An oil can sits on the steps and an owl sleeps in the oak tree.

Pp Albert B. Cub has just parachuted out of a plane with propellers toward a place with apartment buildings and a supermarket. A photographer is taking a photograph or picture of something, but it is not Zebra. What a sight! I hope she doesn't miss that shot. A painter is painting a house with paint. He uses a paintbrush. Things are pink and purple, and there are pale and bright colors all around. A man puffs contentedly on his pipe as he admires his plant. He has a patch on his sweater, and a plate is on the table. Near the dining table hangs a painting of a panda. In the window of the apartment below, a boy plays the piano. I think he is practicing. His parrot listens. A car is parked on the street below. It has pneumatic tires. A boy eats a popsicle while a policeman or patrolman patrols the neighborhood. Just a little bit of his pistol shows. A girl hops along on a pogo stick. Another girl walks a puppy. What a lot of people! Each person is doing something. The priest is listening to the lady. He holds his prayerbook in his hand. Which finger is his pinkie? The lady has a pillbox hat and a purse. A man and woman are crossing the street. They look proud and happy. They must be the parents of the baby who is sucking the pacifier. On the street are two pigeons. One is puffing and pouting. In the supermarket a man is pushing a pushcart. He has a package of oatmeal, among other things. There is a butcher who sells pork sausages, and a poster with a picture of a pig on it. There are potatoes, peaches, plums, and pears in the bins, but there is no zebra.

Qq Continuing his quest, Albert calls on the Queen. She is resting in bed, reading a book with a question mark in its title. She has a quilt made up of quadrilaterals and triangles. Quadrilaterals have four sides. A little quail perches on the windowsill watching Albert eagerly quaff something cool and liquid from a quart pitcher. He is exceedingly thirsty. On the wall hangs a picture of Cupid with his arrows in a quiver. The frame is in the shape of a quatrefoil. It is a pretty shape, like a four-petalled flower. Outdoors, a string quartet plays.

Rr Up goes Albert on a red rocket. Was it built especially for him? It has his initials on it. It is raining raindrops. The rain falls everywhere but it will not stop Albert. He is resolute in his determination to recover his zebra. But look! There is a rainbow in the sky. A child in a raincoat with boots and umbrella walks by the wall made of rocks. In the distance are railroad tracks. On the roof of a house a rat runs away with a ring. In the house, dry and cozy, a girl with ribbons on her braids reads a book about a rooster. There is a radiator and a radio, and a picture on the wall shows someone in a

rocking chair or rocker. In the next room a man is watching a horse race on television. Above him hangs a picture of a rabbit in a tulip garden. Roses grow on a rosebush in the yard next door. Inside that house a woman with a rolling pin is making piecrust or cookies. The refrigerator is behind her. In the next room there is a rock group. Upstairs in the window is a rosebud in a vase. A robin is on the roof. He will sing when the sun comes out. Who is that speeding away in his racing car with the Roman numeral six on it? Is it a robber? Should Albert run after him?

Ss Swimming in the sea, Albert searches on. No, I am mistaken, he is only resting at the seashore, for his clothes are on the sand. Someone is searching for something for he is staring into his spyglass. He sees the seagoing ship that has smoke coming out of its smokestack. The portholes look like spots from here. His skin is sunburned. No wonder, for the sun is in the sky. A small sailboat sails by. It has one sail, spars, and sides, a rudder and tiller to steer with, and a sheet to hold the sail. Someone is sailing the boat, which is named "Stella." On the shingle roof of the stand with a sign, a seagull stands. At the stand, someone is selling soda to a girl in a striped swimsuit. She has also bought a hot dog, which is a sort of sausage. There is salt and pepper made of specks, and a spoon. A stilt is behind the girl. It lives along the shore. Some seashells are there, too. A sailor stands. He has a bottle of soda and a straw to sip it. His shirt has stripes and a star. Below on the beach people are sunbathing. A young man is eating a sandwich and reading a story. The rest of his lunch is in the sack. Whose surfboard is that? A boy with stars on his bathing suit is building something in the sand. He has a shovel and a sandpail with a seahorse painted on it. Why isn't he afraid of that striped serpent smiling on the sand? It is only a plastic sea serpent. It is a toy and it belongs to the little girl in the sunbonnet. Her mother, who sits on a towel, has suntan lotion and sunglasses, and someone has left a pair of shoes, which are sneakers, and a pair of socks on the beach. A girl in a shirt and shorts and sandals is running somewhere. She pays no attention to the skindiver who has just come out of the surf with the waves and seaweed. He is carrying a snorkel and spear. Is the girl running because she sees Zebra?

Tt Albert is far from the sea now. He is in the desert, in Texas. A man in a toque is serving him a bowl of chili. His thumb is on the edge of the bowl. I see two stools. They turn.

Albert is on one of them. It is twelve o'clock and time for lunch. A family of tourists is leaving the table. There is a tumbler and a tablecloth on the table. The father, who is wearing a turtleneck shirt, is taller than the mother and the son has a tennis racket. The trim on the door and windows of the adobe house is turquoise blue. Through the window we see a man in a tie talking on the telephone. A sign tells that soda is twenty cents. A tomato is ripening on the window sill. A tree with a trunk grows near the house. The water tap is dripping. Three chickens peck in the yard. Some children are playing with toys. There is a train, a tank, a tiger, and a trumpet. A toad and a terrier and a tortoise join the fun. The terrier has a collar and a tag. The little girl who is twirling a top is barefoot. Her ten toes show. A cowboy trots by on his horse. The horse has teeth and the cowboy has a ten-gallon hat. A turkey struts under the tree, and the cactus behind the turkey has thorns. Towels hang from the line and a tricycle is by the post. Off in the distance a truck with thick tires drives by. It is a moving van from The Thousand Mile Movers. Albert has traveled much more than a thousand miles, but, poor, tired traveler, he has not seen or heard anything of Zebra.

Uu Unicorns are magical beasts with a unique horn. Perhaps this unicorn with his horn pointing up will use his magic to take Albert to Zebra. Albert carries an umbrella, and sits under it. The moon rises; an underwing moth flits by. A uranium hunter, in his underwear of boxer shorts and undershirt, carrying a ukulele and a basket of kitchen utensils, finds a piece of uranium. A utility pole is next to the gentleman with the geiger counter.

Vv A Viking ship is taking Albert on its voyage. It is filled with Vikings. The Vikings wear vests. One is reading a volume of Virgil. The Roman numeral for five is V. The Viking wears a viper around his arm. Albert B. Cub, in his cap with a visor, is carrying a valise. He looks nervous as the ship sails past the vortex. Ships can be sucked down into a vortex. Vikings, beware! Has the magic unicorn taken Albert back to an earlier time? Is that vineyard with vines bearing violet grapes the land of the poet Virgil? An Ionic column lies broken. Its capital has spiral volutes. Someone is walking across a viaduct. A donkey, not a zebra, follows him. Will the volcano with its fiery vermilion-colored crater and foul-smelling vapors erupt in violence? I hope not. Sail on, Albert B. Cub.

Ww Weeping, wailing, and filled with woe, Albert waits on a wall under a waning moon. A whippoorwill waits with him. A wolf howls near a well with a winch and bucket with a handle. Is it a wishing well? If so, has Albert made a wish? An owl, wings outstretched, flies overhead. Far off, a wagon with wheels goes home. A whale is in the water and so is a walrus with whiskers and wrinkles. The waves wash in on the shore and, woeful as Albert feels, others are happy. A bride, a young wife in white, walks with her groom in his waistcoat. She is a woman. He holds her hand; they both have waists and wrists. The groom wears a wristwatch. What a wonderful day this is for them; it is their wedding day. If only Albert could find his dear Zebra. He could be happy, too.

Xx Exhausted and feeling poorly, Albert consults the well-known Dr. Xavier Ramirez. The doctor, who relaxes by playing the xylophone between patients, assures him he is in good health, only tired and depressed. Sadly, Albert studies an X ray of a zebra. Can it be his friend? But no, the doctor tells him it is an X ray taken long ago. On the walls hang two pictures. One is of a Xiphias, or swordfish. The other is a seascape with a xebec riding the waves.

Yy On goes Albert, scarcely noticing his surroundings. He wears his yachting cap less jauntily; his feet are tired. Two youngsters walk along. One yawns, the other has a yo-yo. A young woman practices yoga. Is she a yogi? Her yarn is in her knitting bag. A Yorkshire terrier walks on a leash. A man sits on a park bench eating his lunch of yogurt and a hard-boiled egg with a yellow yolk. What is that yak doing there? Albert does not know, nor does he care. He has not yet found Zebra.

Zz The full moon is rising to its zenith, and oh, what a joyous night it is! Albert has found Zebra! Where? In the zoo, where the lion lies sleeping. Hear him snore, "Zzzzz!" He does not hear the zebra leave. How did he get there? I do not know, nor does Albert. Only Zebra knows, and tomorrow he will tell Albert his tale. But now he is content to nibble a zinnia that Albert has brought him. Albert's jacket zipper is zipped tight to keep him warm in the evening air. Have you noticed the shape of the letter Z? It is a zigzag.

Good-bye and good night, Albert B. Cub and Zebra. May you never be parted again.